America's

Internal

Enemy

The Dividers

Shantanu Kamat

1

Dedicated to

The greatest country on the earth, for accepting me, giving me a lot and making me a better person.

America will never be destroyed from the outside. If we falter and lose our freedoms, it will be because we destroyed ourselves.

----- Abraham Lincoln

*C*hapters

*A*ppendix

Preface

Where there's a will there's a way. When I was working in Silicon Valley, California, my company had a very meticulously and proactively maintained information section, for the company customers. It was called 'known problems and solutions'. It gave customers the information about the known problems, and the solutions to address those problems. Every group in the company worked in harmony, to provide these solutions to the customers. It was a united front on the part of the company. The reason is that all the groups had a common interest, in the betterment and success of the company.

Today, America is aware of the problems it is facing and also knows what the solutions are. Unlike any other country in the world, America is still that imperial force, which can easily solve these problems on it's own. This nation has some of the brightest and the most capable people in the government coupled with the most productive brains in almost every part of the industry. It also has a strong legal system and a very powerful media that can keep the politicians on their toes, for doing their jobs. All America needs, is the will in their politicians and the media, to really fix the problems.

In the 2012 Presidential elections, Romney, the Presidential candidate of Abraham Lincoln's party was polling at almost 0%, with the African Americans and the lowest ever, among the Hispanics. On the other hand, Obama was polling the lowest ever, among the white voters, in the history of the Presidential candidates. This extremity has put America on a very dangerous path, as the Party line division, seems to be clearly along the racial lines.

Similar party line divide, is seen between women voters versus men voters, young voters versus older voters and married people versus the unmarried people. This electoral polarization, is actually taking America back in time.

Division hurts every community, no matter how invincible the community might appear. In my country of birth India, when the British arrived to conquer the country, they made the neighboring kingdoms fight against each other, through their technique of 'divide and rule'. They divided people along the regional lines, racial lines and religious lines. As a result, only a few hundred thousand Brits ruled millions of people in India. India was able to regain the independence, only when the entire nation united behind Mahatma Gandhi.

Currently, we see that the Republican Party is divided between the right wing, non compromising extremists and the moderates. This division, done quite deliberately, by a handful of few, has left the Republican Party in peril. At the same time, the venomous hatred is being spewed towards the liberal America and the Democratic President, by the same people, causing the unprecedented division between the liberal and the conservative America.

This division has reached such precarious levels in 2012, that in the Republican primaries, almost 70% of the Republican voters voted against Mitt Romney, and then in the Presidential elections, they supported Mitt Romney only because they wanted to vote against Barack Obama. The Democratic voter base was not so enthusiastic about Obama and his record. But they came out to vote because they could not possibly see, the right wing extremism and hostility, in power. Such disdain for the other side is very counterproductive, to the progress of the nation as a whole.

This division is hurting America, a lot more than any external force.

----- An immigrant's perspective.

1) The greatest country in the world

"I have been driven to my knees, many times, because of the overwhelming conviction, that I have nowhere else to go".

Barack Obama was quoting Abraham Lincoln, in the 2012 Democratic National Convention. Abraham Lincoln, a Republican, who abolished slavery, which perhaps has a lot to do with Barack Obama, a Democrat, being elected the first African American President of America. America, being the first majority white country, to elect a black President.

Sometimes, reality is more stunning than the imagination. When a person comes to America from the outside world, imagining what America would be like, and then stays in America, observes it to every minute detail, the only conclusion the person will come to is, America is a country where imagination has been exceeded, and is turned into the reality.

If you saw Barack Obama and Mitt Romney speeches, at the 2012 Al Smith Memorial Foundation Dinner in New York, you would notice the two exceptionally intelligent, scholastic and extremely successful self made men. Both looking beyond Presidential, taking humorous cracks at each other, using the material written by the highest caliber comedy writers. These two people are the elites of the elite class. The best of Harvard Law vs Harvard Business. A credit to their professions. Only Americans, can boast of these two elites, as the Presidential candidates of their major parties. And the success stories of their country.

The country with the most advanced technical industry in the world, the greatest universities and institutions in the world, the greatest innovators in the world, the greatest financial industry in the world, the greatest entertainment industry in the world, the greatest celebrities in the world, the greatest military in the world, the most charitable country in the world, the greatest sports nation in the world, the greatest marketing force in the world, the country of the greatest cities and landmarks in the world. You name it and America has it. I am sure that the previous great empires, like the great Roman empire and the great British empire, probably did not have it all, at once, and that too on such a grand scale, in their prime for those times.

But the single most distinguishing factor of the American greatness is the character and the nature of the American people, which is a mix of friendliness, politeness, honesty and broad mindedness. Of course, I am talking about the solid majority of Americans. And it is my firm belief that no one can observe and appreciate this better, than an immigrant, who has immigrated to the US, especially from a poor third world country.

Every country has a small population of conceited, xenophobic, unfriendly and even the racist people. And I am sure America has it's share of those.

However, the majority of the Americans are by far the most admirable people in the world.

Initially, I was truly surprised that Americans do not show any superiority complex, about the greatness and wealth of their country, to the people visiting from much poorer countries. To go a step beyond, over the time, they openly embrace you as their own citizen, irrespective of your color, mannerism and religion. I have visited enough countries in the world, and have gone out of my way to interact with the people, to observe their behavior. I don't think any other country is, so genuinely open and friendly to the outsiders.

Well, you can always say that America has been the country of immigrants. But to use this reason to discredit the Americans, as the nicest people, is a huge injustice to them. I am not just talking about the liberal America, where I spent all my years, and where the majority of the immigrants arrive. Even in the most conservative state of Kansas, almost all the people I ran into were by far, the friendliest and the nicest. Loved Kansas.

This tells me that this nice behavior has to be something, well beyond being just the country of immigrants. Majority of the country is still white Caucasian and pretty isolated from the world. They have what they need in their own country. I think this good natured behavior comes from the fact that the country is very religious. It does not have the aristocratic class system like Europe has. And more importantly, they are very successful collectively as a nation, which makes them the least insecure people in the world.

And since the country is just over two hundred years old, the Americans do not live in the past and do not have the phony pride about their culture. They take pride in and abide by their constitution which is written by very progressive and the most intelligent people of those times.

As a consequence, in terms of broad mindedness, friendliness and honesty, Americans have matured on average, more than any other nation in the world, despite being a very conservative nation.

But in the last few years, in such a great country of friendly, well spoken and charitable people, we have started observing a disturbing trend that most of the Americans can see quite prominently. Specially in the election season. Politically, it has become a divided nation, a polarized nation and a disappointed nation, according to the majority of Americans.

Not agreeing with the opposition party agenda is a very common trend. So is, disliking the political leaders of the opposition party, and expressing dissent for their policies. But the division between the blue states and the red states has now reached culmination. Day by day, there is growing aversion and hysteria about the other side, and to such an extent that, 'not voting for the other side' has become the impetus, behind people supporting their own party/ candidate. People have started ignoring the voting record and the credibility of their own political party and the candidates. Where does so much antipathy for the other party arise, in the nation of the friendliest and the most charitable people on earth?

It comes from a very few and powerful people in the media, who have interest in causing this division for the purpose of making money. They are doing it, despite knowing that it is hurting the country. They achieve their objective of division, by spreading misinformation and inciting hatred towards the other side. By using incendiary language and hyperbole, while teaching their viewers, how compromise of any kind with the other side, is against their principles. Many opportunist politicians, who are just hiding behind this powerful media, have now started exploiting this division, for their political expediency.

America, despite being the richest and the most resourceful country in the world, among the developed nations, has the highest income inequality, the highest child poverty rate, the highest child obesity rate and the highest imprisonment rate.

America spends more money on health care and education, than any other country in the world. But ranks pretty low on the returns, for both these crucial necessities.

America's military empire is doing nation building in Iraq and Afghanistan. The empire, on which America spends more money, than the next 15 nations combined, 13 of which are America's allies. Meanwhile America's own infrastructure, ranks 22nd in the world. The crumbling infra structure, that was exposed in hurricanes Katrina and Sandy.

These problems are worsening day by day. The division in the country, caused quite deliberately by a few, is depriving the American middle class people of their own country's resources, and is adding more hardships to their everyday lives. For example, in the amount of money that was spent on Iraq war, every uninsured in America could have received free health care. Plenty of such examples can be found.

Everyday American life is now becoming a combination of the rising costs, reducing benefits and growing insecurity. The divided country will never be able to address these issues. This is why America needs the media and the politicians who unite the nation.

Tragically, quite the opposite is true.

2) Government, Capitalism and Individual Responsibility

Both Barack Obama and Mitt Romney spoke eloquently and appeared very likable at the 2012 Al Smith Memorial Foundation Dinner. But I am not sure how many voters, appreciated the candidate of the opposition party.

Perhaps, it is not the fault of these voters. As soon as these two got off the stage, and went back to campaigning, their slogans changed into Romney saying, bad government has strangled job creators and small businesses. Obama saying, rich people and Wall Street are playing by different set of rules, to hurt the middle class.

The reason why these two candidates are using these slogans is, because the media and the politicians have created these two different images of America. And have taught the people to select only one image that sides with their political affiliation.

In reality, in their current state, neither the American government is bad nor the American capitalism. None of the two, is actually interfering in common man's life that much. If people feel that there is an interference from the bad government, or if they are bearing the brunt of bad capitalism, in reality, there is lot more positive than the negative, to gain from, both the government and the capitalism in America. There is more encouragement, and more helping hand offered by both, in America, than in any other nation in the world.

The reason I am saying this, is because both of them have helped me enormously. And that too, despite me being an average immigrant, from a third world country. I am indebted to both of them, to a very big extent.

All I had to do was to show the willingness to help myself, by grabbing the available opportunities. And try not to blame anything else, for my current situation. America had plenty to offer to me, when I moved here, and still has plenty to offer to every person in America, let alone the American citizens.

I applied to a few universities in the US after my Bachelors degree in Physics, in India. I was well aware that I would not be able to pay the entire tuition fees in the top and expensive universities, whether or not I get an admission there. Hence, I applied to the average / decent universities. California State University, Fresno, gave me an admission and the teaching assistantship for the master's program. This is a government funded university, and my first paycheck came from the state of California. This was the first helping hand to me. A helping hand that came from the American government, which is currently demonized in the conservative media.

Most of my American class mates got jobs in the defense companies, based on their Physics major. But

I did not have the US citizenship for these positions. I realized that Physics major is not going to get me a job. Only thing that I needed, was the willingness to educate myself in the field that can give me a job. Deep down, I always knew that in the land of opportunities, there was no shortage of options. I decided to take classes in the Electrical Engineering field, and also targeted the Silicon Valley, the technology capital of the world, as a place where I can look for a job.

The same government funded state university chain, offered me a chance to move to San Jose State University, in the heart of Silicon Valley. That too, on the Open University program, which charged me only $1000 for the semester, to take the classes in the Electrical Engineering department.

Later on, the government issued me a one year work permit, called 'Practical Training' to find the job of my liking in any company, before the company can file for my permanent work permit.

Isn't this more than one could ask for? Which other country would grant such opportunities, to an average foreign student, at such low costs? And if the foreign students can get so many opportunities in the US, why can't Americans get them? And in this case for me, why was the government, bad after all?

Later on, I was fortunate enough to get a decent salary job, by the standards of high tech industry. Our company's products were used to design semiconductor chips, which are used in a wide range of industries. I had the privilege of working with some of the brightest people in the world. I never felt that they did not deserve the success or the wealth they earned. In fact we were proud of them. I don't think anyone hates success in America. Neither the conservatives do, nor the liberals.

And about the company management, and the investors, so called rich people; they had interest in nothing but higher profits. What's wrong? We knew about this, even before joining the company, and if we were to complain about it, we should have chosen a different job. In fact, this drive for higher profits is what is driving the growth and the success.

Both of my companies had offices in India, where US jobs were sent. But that was to increase the productivity and the efficiency. After all, business is not a charity, which has a moral obligation to keep the jobs in the US. The jobs for which, the company has to bear a much higher cost per employee.

But don't get me wrong, both my companies kept enough employees in America and treated them well. Hence, we realized that if we wanted to keep our jobs in the America, it is our responsibility to be one of those workers, and work towards being retained for these positions in America. There is a new myth being created in the conservative media that, liberals hate rich people and their success. Not true.

Granted, in the recent years, government has done big blunders and has done lot of wasteful spending; for example, going to Iraq war. Unregulated capitalism has also reached the nadir of unethical business practices; for example the mortgage crisis, banking collapse, etc. But such bad steps are taken against the middle class interests, all over the world, and to a much worse extent. Americans are very fortunate that even today, they are in a country, where the government and the corporations are both, in a much better position, to help the life and the success of a common man. A lot more than anywhere else in the world.

Problem today is that some people on the both sides are not willing to take the individual responsibility, and are being taught by the cunning politicians, that somehow people are perfect. And the blame for their economic problem falls on someone else, needless to say the opposition party. If the voters of both the parties take a good look at their candidates, Obama and Romney; both are self made men and both are helped tremendously by the government, as well as the private sector. In fact there isn't a country on this planet, where government and the corporations, work as closely as in America.

During the campaign season, on Romney's and Obama's Facebook pages, people were complaining how things are not getting better for them, how they have lost their houses, how they have not been able to find the work for a long time, how new college grads are having to move back, into their parent's houses, and so on.

The bitter truth answer to that is, too many Americans had it too easy, for too long. I know that, this is not a popular answer, but it is a new reality. It is very much understandable, why Americans are feeling this way, and are wondering whose fault it is. For a long time, they were the citizens of a wealthy country, when the economy was not global and the manufacturing was local. It is like being born in a very rich household.

So many people from the baby boomer generation, without a competitive technical college degree, perhaps with a help of a 2 year training course, and that too in the field of their liking, held lifelong jobs. They had sufficiently good/ decent salaries, and the health care coverage paid by the employer. Then they retired, with good social security and Medicare benefits, for the rest of their lives.

But that was never a reality.

That was a privilege and a good fortune, because they were the citizens of America. Rarely in any other country, this much amount of luxury is offered, despite people working more hard. Rarely in any other country, you get to choose the major you like, and yet retain the job for the rest of your life, with decent salary, great benefits, and also the best standard of living in the world.

But now, in the global economy, when the jobs are shipped to low waged countries, it time to take tougher individual responsibility. Time to see if the major you choose, is going to give you a job. Even today, less than 15% of Americans choose Engineering, Medicine, Law and Finance as their career majors. These are the only majors, which will most likely get you a good paying, permanent job, which is least likely to be shipped out side.

Americans will have to change the perspective, to align with the rest of the world, even if their country is still much superior to the rest of the world. This does not mean, America is on decline. This, just means that the gap between America and the rest of the world has shrunk.

This is not something that people like to hear. But the fact of the matter is, every Indian/ Chinese student I know, who has come to the US in this bad Bush/ Obama economy, has found at least one and in some cases more than one, highly paid jobs, out of school. And that too, despite having to get their work permits approved. The work permit gets approved, only if no qualified Americans, can be found to do these jobs.

When 23 million Americans are either unemployed or underemployed, why are there almost 3 million job vacancies open, even today in America, which can not be filled? The answer to that is, the skill sets of these 23 million people, are not matching the skills required to perform these open jobs.

American corporations are sitting on the record amount of cash, and are showing the Wall Street the record amount of profits. Why aren't they hiring, causing reduction in unemployment? The reason is, the corporations are able to achieve their objectives, without hiring more workers.

Is this the fault of the government? Is this the fault of the corporations? Is this fault of Bush, Obama or Romney? Of course not. This is just the new reality.

But no politician and the media is telling this to the American people. On the contrary, they misguide the American people by saying that it is someone else's fault. It is the fault of the other party and the dysfunctional Washington. One side is blaming this on the government, and the other side is blaming this on unregulated Wall Street.

This blame game is very beneficial to the opportunists in both the parties, and their media mouth pieces, who are serving their own interests.

Of course, this does not mean that every media mouth piece is deceitful, or the media mouth pieces on both the sides, are being equally cynical. But a few in the conservative media, on purpose, are targeting the low information, vulnerable audience and are keeping them in dark, by spreading a lot of misinformation, through politically crass language. They are carrying out a continuous tirade, against the other political party and it's President, causing the greatest political division in generations.

Fox news and talk radio are the masters of this strategy. And while doing so, they knowingly overlook the real interest of their own viewers and the real interest of their own political party.

The real interest actually, is the need for compromise and bipartisanship.

3) The dividers

"Is this just math that you do as a Republican, to make your self feel better, or is this real?"!!!!

Baffled Fox news anchor Megyn Kelly, finally lost it and asked this question to the Republican guru Karl Rove. He was questioning the Fox News call, to declare Ohio for President Obama, based on their estimated 99.99% chance, on the election night 2012. Karl Rove, the smartest guy alive in the American politics, who deep down knew, that Ohio is gone for the night.

'Fair & Balanced'. What a dynamic slogan for a news organization! In our childhood, we were told that more corrupt the politician is, whiter the clothes he wears. Fox news having this high moral slogan, reminds me exactly of these corrupt to the core politicians.

For now, one can ignore whether the TV show hosts like Bill Oreilly, Sean Hannity, Greta Van Sustern, Glenn Beck (former host), etc are biased or not. Just take a look at the list of the analysts, contributors and frequent guests.

Karl Rove: The deputy chief of staff of Bush White House and the legendary architect of the administration

Sarah Palin: Former Republican VP nominee

Newt Gingrich: Republican speaker of the house and the Republican presidential nominee

Mike Huckabee: Republican governor and the Republican presidential nominee

John Bolton: Republican U.S. ambassador to the United Nations nominated by George Bush

Donald Trump: Self proclaimed Republican presidential nominee, and a devoted anti Obama non sense promoter.

Is it a coincidence that all of them belong to only one party? Does Fox news have the equivalent influential people from the Democratic Party, to counter the undisputed opinions of these stalwarts? Where is the fairness and where is the balance? In that case, how the slogan 'Fair & Balanced', is not a lie?

There is a big portion of the American population that identifies itself as Republican. They will resolutely vote Republican, no matter what. Reasons for this party affiliation might be several. 1) This is a party of Abraham Lincoln. 2) Having a belief that being a Republican is same as being a real heartland American. Consequently believing that heartland America is the real America. Also, the belief that people in heartland America are the only people, who believe in American exceptionalism 3) Being Republican means being a patriot. Since the majority of the Army also votes Republican 4) Being Republican means being a values voter (traditional family, religious beliefs) and being for individual liberty 5) Being Republican means being for capitalism 6) Being a Republican means being fiscally conservative, being responsible with government spending, supporting less government involvement in life, etc.

In short, being a Republican means standing for something. They also believe that the liberals or the Democrats don't stand for these values, or in fact don't stand for anything.

Fox news and talk radio have targeted this demographic, as their audience, and have been successful in convincing them a step further; that the liberals and the Democrats, are antithetical to these values (6 points above).

One would be surprised to find out, how such a big chunk of population in the most advanced country in the world, can fall for such propaganda engines, like Fox news and talk radio. But it is not that difficult to understand.

The heartland of the US is still very isolated from the rest of the world. Heartland population, is still a majority white Caucasian and religious Christian population. And even if America is the most advanced country in the world, majority of the innovation, industry is located in the coastal America. Majority of the immigrants as well, migrate to the coastal states or to the big cities of the red states, which keeps their interaction with the heartland very less.

With so many immigrants like Hispanics, Chinese, Indians, who also happen to be colored, pouring into the country, it is only a human nature to dislike the change. Also the area of the country, where the change is visible. In addition, people in these states, being open to, and being flexible on the social issues, like homosexuality, abortion, female equality, brings further dislike, as the heartland people are more religious and family values people. Since the message of this changing America, resonates very well with the heartland, Fox news and talk radio, make use of it, to create the political divide.

Their job is to cleverly convey, that this change is actually degradation.

And who better to do it, than the polarizing and divisive Fox News analysts like Newt Gingrich, who has compared Obama administration's damage to

America to the one caused by Nazis to Germany. Sarah Palin, who has called small town America, "real" and "pro American" place. Add to which, side shows like Donald Trump, who for the last 4 years have been questioning the birth place, of the first black President, who had a Kenyan father of Islamic faith.

These analysts, coupled with their talk show hosts like Sean Hannity, Glenn Beck, Bill O'Reilly and Greta Van Susteren, who have mastered the art of the selective anti liberal phony outrages, phony conservatism, and phony patriotism, is the match made in heaven, to capture the dislike of the liberal, Democratic America, and turn it into the hatred towards it.

Fox news has a companion in talk radio. Rush Limbaugh and company. Their combined job is to scare, working class white and religious people, and make them believe, that their country is changing and retrogressing, in values and standards. In short, this is not their same America, which was once a perfect country. And if the President of this liberal, Democratic America is African American, who can be labeled as a big government spender, a socialist, a Marxist, then it is easier to covey the change, and the retrogression.

Majority of these low information voters, start finding some truth and logic to this propaganda, after hearing it again and again, every day. Eventually, they get addicted to it, because they get to hear what they like. This locks the viewership of Fox news, Talk Radio. Increases their revenues and ratings

Meanwhile, the disdain for the liberal or the Democratic America is so much embedded into their minds, that any kind of 'compromise' with the Democratic ideas and policies, becomes an inconceivable notion. Any policy proposal by the most hated President, even if it is the food stamps, which grew the most under the Republican President, can be used as a sarcastic campaign slogan, against the same President.

In reality, America is changing and also retrogressing to some extent. Middle class is shrinking and is finding it harder to make ends meet. Salaries are stagnant but costs of living are rising. But not for the reasons, told by Fox news and talk radio. The real reasons will not be told. The real culprits, will not be exposed. Because the reality is, a bitter pill to swallow. One of the realities, which is causing this retrogression, is the inability of the two sides to work with each other. A value nurtured by the Fox news and talk radio.

The next step of hate game is the scare tactic. Appeal to the race, and somehow insinuate that the Black President inherently hates white America.

If I go into every example, of how Fox news and talk radio, achieve this hate and scare game, it will take me a whole new book. Hence, following are only some of the countless quotes and points, from just the two people; Glenn Beck and Rush Limbaugh, who lead this 'Anti Obama, the black leader of the bad liberal America' crusade. Time and again, appealing to the race.

Rush Limbaugh:

- They are finally hearing me, he is an angry black guy

- I want this President to fail

- We got the militant black reaction

- Basically we got a community organizer in action last night

- He is fanning the flames of race

- You have a black President trying to destroy a white police man

- When Colin Powell (An American patriot and a Bush government loyal) endorsed Obama, Rush Limbaugh screamed into this micro phone saying, this is 'only' about race.

Glenn Beck:

- This guy has real issues with race

- This President has a deep seeded hatred for the white people or the white culture

- This guy I believe is a racist

How will this not incite hatred, in the low information white working class viewers? Viewers, who already dislike the change in their country? Viewers, who are losing their jobs to the colored people?

How will this not divide heartland America from the liberal America?

And if the timid Republican candidates like Mitt Romney, who show the cowardice not to stand up to these voices, how will it not drive non whites away from the GOP, in the Presidential elections?

Is it a surprise that, 2012 Presidential elections, were the most racially divided, in the modern history of the US?

The next category of division is the anti American agenda. The goal here is that, those who can not be swayed away by race and changing demographics, against Obama's Democrats, can be swayed by appeal to national patriotism. Needless to say, the phony patriotism created through distortion.

Portray Obama and his henchmen, as somehow non Americans. Starting from giving credence to the people, questioning his birth in the US, questioning his Christian faith by referring to his Muslim father, constant references to his middle name Hussein, making claims of Obama not believing in American exceptionalism, Obama not believing in stronger

America, to making an indirect suggestions of Obama having anti American feelings.

For example, criticizing Obama for an apology tour based on his Cairo speech. When, on the contrary, Israeli prime minister Mr. Natanyahu, said the following about the same speech, "Obama is the first US President to stand in front of the Arab nation, and tell them that Israel is America's best friend".

Later on, a new ridiculous notion was invented that "Obama threw Israel under the bus" when Obama took the same stand, taken by Bush and Clinton, on 1965 borders, with mutually agreed swaps, by both Israel and Palestine.

In short, somehow project that Obama, a Muslim father's son, is the first President to be more sympathetic to the Islamic world, and more hostile to America's ally Israel.

In reality and by contrast, following is what Ehud Barak, the Israeli Defense Minister said,

"But I should tell you honestly that this administration under President Obama, is doing in regard to our security, more than anything that I can remember in the past."

Is this called throwing Israel under the bus?

Israeli Prime Minister Mr. Natanyahu said, the following on Sean Hannity Show, "Israeli – American security cooperation is at an all time high. We just had a revolutionary development now, in military history, to develop an anti missile system".

The same Sean Hannity, who has spent countless hours, thrashing President Obama for being a bad President for Israel's security and an overall weak and incompetent President.

How disingenuous? How unpatriotic? How shameful? How cowardly?

In reality, actually it is the Fox news and the extremists in the Republican Party, who have thrown the image of 'America – Israel friendship', under the bus.

Isn't this dividing America from it's best friend Israel, who is all alone in the troubled region?

I don't think even America's enemies are so low in morals. And the viewers are supposed to believe, that Fox news and talk radio hosts are patriots!

Further, Obama is criticized for things, as trivial as not being able to bring home the Olympics. On the other hand, if he actually wins the Nobel Peace Prize, then Nobel Peace prize committee is criticized, for awarding it to an incompetent President. In short, if Obama fails, it is his fault. If Obama wins, it is someone else being unfair.

In short, always root against the American President and portray him as a symbol of American mediocrity, whose values are antithetical to the values of heartland America. The patriotic heartland values of American exceptionalism.

A simple suggestion for common good, about healthy eating, becomes government interference and a nanny state.

This new cynical and unpatriotic propaganda engine has captured hold of the Tea Party, and a big part of the GOP. They have no interest in the betterment of the Tea Party or the Republican party or the nation.

They have interest in only one thing. The division, that gives them high ratings and unprecedented high revenues.

They never tell Tea Party, what really is driving up the national debt, and who actually have spent lot more of their tax payer money, under which President they are paying the lowest taxes, what is the voting records of the Tea Party favorites, under which President, America's favorability has risen in Europe, etc.

You will also, never hear about income inequality in America. You will never hear about better environment. You will also never hear about growing obesity and the need to eat healthier. In conclusion, nothing beneficial for your real life.

In short, the cynicism playing to the ignorance.

4) Ignorance and cynicism

If a country that has led the world, in pretty much every scientific and technological invention, for the last 100 years, but does not believe in global warming in the 21st century, despite being hit by growing number of hurricanes, and if a country which is home to the brightest minds in the world, in every possible field of humanity, but has to listen to Sarah Palin for the betterment of the country, then certain section of this great nation, is deliberately kept in ignorance, by some cynics.

Some members of the Tea Party like to claim, that the Tea Party existed for almost a decade. But the fact is that majority of Americans, did not hear about them, till January of 2009. Tea Party agenda as well, is very simple. They don't like government spending, borrowing money and the national debt. They also like low taxes. This sounds morally high, constitutional and quite patriotic.

But the most perplexing part is, why did they hold their first protest in February 2009? Why do they believe, that government spending has gone up for the first time, after January of 2009? Why do they believe that taxes have gone up, after January of 2009? Why do they believe that their individual liberty is under threat, after January of 2009, for the first time?

Something is ought to be wrong here. Why wasn't the first rally held in 2001, when the Afghanistan war was started without being paid for? Granted, that the war was a response to 9/11, Tea Party can be given a break. What about the two Bush tax cuts, without paying for them, when CBO said that they would add to the national deficit? Later, what about the Iraq war in 2003, without paying for it? What about the prescription drug program, the largest overhaul of Medicare, in the public health program's 38-year history, without paying for it? And most importantly what about the TARP, the first tax funded government bailout in 2008, that costed $700 billion plus of the tax payer money? What about the first portion of the auto bailout in 2008?

I am not even talking about the priceless loss of life, of the American troops in Iraq. Not one protest by the tea party 'patriots', for the loss of lives, of the American troops? For the war, that was later proven to be a on a bad intelligence? Not one protest, for using American tax payer money for rebuilding Iraq? Seriously? Is this Tea Party patriotism?

They waited for 8 long years for their first protest, and that too, against the stimulus bill of 2009 that had almost 50% tax breaks? The stimulus bill, that was issued because America was losing 800,000 jobs a month? Against the stimulus bill, that according to Congressional Budget Office, saved a million jobs? Against a successful bailout of the car industry, America's pride, that went from being on the brink of shutting down, to GM being world's number 1 car maker again?

How can the timing of the first protest be justifiable?

There are only three possibilities. 1) Extreme ignorance 2) Extreme partisanship, which means selective recollection of the bad things, happening only under the watch of the opposition party, 3) Racism. Thanks to the newly elected black President, whose American and Christian identity, can be questioned!

Then, as a solution to these new found tax and spend problems, the Tea Party started supporting Republican Party. The Republican Party that has spent record amount of money, and accrued record amount of deficits, by blowing up the surplus, between the years 2000-2008.

All 139 congressmen/ senators, supported by the Tea Party in 2010 midterm elections, were for the GOP. On the contrary, the Tea Party members despised and protested against the President, under whom taxes are the lowest, in our lifetimes. The President under whom, the new federal spending has increased, by the lowest margins ever.

And guess who the Tea Party loves. Paul Ryan. The person, who voted for each and every Bush spending program, without paying for it, and even without accounting for it.

This is nothing but 1) hatred/racism, 2) partisanship and 3) ignorance in that order.

Could there have been a more ideal target for Fox news, than a group of people, with the combination of these three qualities? Within the matter of days, the Tea Party was taken over by spiritual leaders of Fox news, talk radio and the crazy wing of the Republican Party.

A breeding ground for division, hatred and partisanship.

This gave rise to a new narrative, for the next three years, or at least till the end of Obama's first term. Government is bad, our freedom is under threat, Obama wants to distribute our wealth, America is going to become a socialist European country like

Greece, Obama does not believe in American exceptionalism, Obama has started war against the Christianity, he is pandering to our enemies and so on.

To summarize, we need to take our country back!

This ignorance and cynicism, has given rise to a troubling trend of staying loyal to the Republican Party, no matter how bad the party's voting record was. No matter what the credibility of the party members is. Next step was an urge, to defend the bad party record and bad politicians, to any extent. And the last step was to blame the other party, for the bad things your own party has done.

In short, the rise of dishonesty.

This dishonesty always existed in the politicians. The ignorance always existed in the voter base. But what has changed for worse in America, and specially the extreme wing of the Republican party, is that political dishonesty has trickled down, among the partisan voters. This is giving the license, to the party politicians and the party mouth pieces, to spread the misinformation and non cooperation to any extent, for scoring the political points. The reason is that the party politicians know, they will get votes from their voter base, no matter what. They will win their district, no matter what. Michele Bachmann, being one of such examples.

This dishonesty, coupled with the strong incendiary language from the myopic right wing politicians, and the conservative media, has permanently damaged the brand of the Republican Party.

The brand has lost the national appeal. The brand that has driven away the moderates, and has taken it's second consecutive, land slide Presidential election beating.

Eventually causing many of the party's moderates to say, "We have to stop being a stupid party".

5) Intentional destruction of the Republican Party

"Oh, I think Mitt Romney is going to win in a land slide". I am quoting a 'default' Fox news analyst here.

Fox news viewers have to ask themselves a simple question, based on the following scenario, also called as reality. Each and every of their analysts and commentators, who were willing to predict the election outcome, predicted either a Romney win or a Romney landslide win. Not one predicted an Obama win. In reality, Obama won in a land slide, winning all the swing states. So the question for the Fox news viewers is, "Are these people all lying to you, or are they all collectively incompetent"? Again, because not one of them, Predicted an Obama win. Even a narrow Obama win.

And if you can not still figure out an answer, then look at their pay rolls. Incompetent people don't make millions of dollars. But the people, who can fool masses, can.

Genius is the first word that comes to mind, when it comes to Fox News and talk radio, no matter how cynical they may sound, and no matter how damaging they may be for their viewers.

After all, they are the inventors of the biased media. The media, that takes side. The media that provides their viewers with the news, "they like to hear". In fact, calling it news, is by itself is an irony. Calling it 'hysterical entertainment' is probably a more appropriate term.

There is a significant amount of GOP voter base that is addicted to this viewership model.

Naturally, to meet this requirement of 'what they like to hear' news, the information becomes misinformation, the liberal America becomes 'non values' America and the democratic President becomes a non traditional President. The misinformation, further extents to, not believing in facts and science, just because the liberal America is abiding by it.

For example, GOP voter base, not believing in global warming, to which about 90% of the scientist in the world, have an accord on. Three GOP Presidential candidates in 2008, did not believe even in the evolution, with a hilarious excuse, "I was not there".

Not to mention, no awareness about the environment killers like cutting trees, usage of plastic bags, coal industry and so on.

This facts free, biased media business model, has been damaging the GOP voter base, in the three major areas.

Values, intellect and demographics.

Damage to the values:

Catastrophic Presidency comes once in a life time, for a mature Democracy like America. But when it comes, it does a lot of short term and permanent damage to the country and to their party.

Jimmy Carter, although not so harmful to the country, although a great humanitarian post Presidency, haunted Democrats for a long time. On the Republican side, unfortunately the Presidency of George Bush and Dick Cheney, did significant damage to the party reputation. Firstly, by setting the historically low bar for the economic calamity. When they left office, American economy was losing 750,000 jobs a month. A disastrous foreign policy, that left America with the lowest approval ratings of all time, in the outside world.

Now, I am not saying this as a Democrat or as a Republican. I also don't blame Bush administration much, for the economic collapse. But, quite obviously, the after effects of this administration on the common man's mind, were perpetual. For the two successive Republican presidential conventions, Bush and Cheney, who were in power till just recently for 8 years, were not present. Not in 2008 and not in 2012. Weren't they expected to play a big supporting role in the convention? Like Bill Clinton did for the Democrats in the same years? This is the after effect of the ongoing drag, of this administration, on the country, and on the current Republican Party.

An oil man and an ex CEO of Halli Burton. When the tragedy of 9/11 happened under their watch, the approval rating of Bush was in 90s. The country could have forgiven them for pretty much anything. Precisely, what they took advantage of.

If you ask any level headed person in the world, including in America, the reason for Iraq invasion, the answer you will get is "oil", and the corporate welfare. Iraq had the second largest oil resource in the world. In the 1991 Gulf war, George W. Bush's father, was successful in getting an American base in Saudi Arabia, the country with the biggest oil resource in the world. In 2003, his son got the base in Iraq. In addition, Halli Burton got a no bid, multi billion contract in Iraq.

This is not a rocket science.

Given the big loss of life, in the eyes of a common man in the world, this was a crime against humanity and an open daylight robbery. In the eyes of Bush administration and the Fox news, this was defending America, spreading freedom/democracy, and the Judeo Christian American values. Bush administration through Fox news and the talk radio propaganda engines, was relentless, in hammering their version of reasons, to the viewers. Kept on defending this war as a value and the necessity. Fresh fear from 9/11, played a big role in America digesting this war.

At the end of the Bush Presidency, this is where the Republican Party voter base, ended up with, in terms of contradicting their values.

The "pro life party" voter base, that fights for the life of an unborn fetus, was responsible for invading a wrong country, through a war, that killed over 3500 of our own soldiers, and over 300,000 Iraqi civilians. Families of these soldiers lost their livelihoods forever. Thousands of Iraqi children became permanently disabled, even before they could step into the adulthood. At the same time, the Fox news, talk radio hosts and analysts were making millions of dollars, selling this war.

People who reelected George Bush ignored this loss of life.

The party of high morals and family values started torturing people in Guantanamo bay Cuba. Not torturing, was considered weak and endangering America. In 2012 GOP primary debates, the death penalty was cheered upon and people without the health insurance, were asked to be left alone to die on the road, if they did not have the health insurance and get hit by a car.

How do the people, who believe in Jesus Christ so much, come to this?

The only justifiable answer is the combination, of narcissism, ignorance, and aversion towards the other side. Justify whatever we do is correct, because we are the perfect people, as taught by Fox news and Rush Limbaugh. And learn to oppose everything that the other side wants to do, even if it means voting against your own principles and interests. If the other side wants to give health insurance to the poor, you oppose it. If the other side wants to close the Guantanamo bay, you oppose it. If other side wants to get out of wars, you call them weak.

This is the evil genius of Fox news and talk radio that has really taken away the "Jesus Christ Values" voters away, from the values of Jesus. Fox news hosts, who claim to be the worshippers of Judeo Christian values, would never ask their voters a simple question,

"Is this what Jesus would do"?

These wars and the tortures have done irreparable damage to the American reputation, in the outside world.

But Fox news and their viewers are already prepared for this. Their take on this is, "Who cares for the world outside"? We are exceptional. America is never wrong, and we will never apologize. Not even for the death of 300.000 civilians, and 3500 of our own soldiers.

'Apology' has become such an 'unconstitutional' word, in the conservative media, that following is what Mitt Romney said about apology.

"We may make mistakes as a nation time to time, and step on other's toes, and we will say sorry for that, but apologizing for America, is something I will never ever do".

Not sure, if this is a line from a comedy movie, or a line from the rally, of the Presidential candidate of Abraham Lincoln's party.

Needless to say, this line was received with cheers by the audience. And this is when one can start questioning the intelligence of the audience.

Damage to the intellect:

Quite understandably, it is a human nature that people feel a little inferior compared to the elites. It is quite natural to find elites overbearing. It is also quite natural, not to identify yourself with the elites. But never before 2008, it was believed in America, that it was bad to be an elite, specially a coastal elite. Never before 2008, it was believed that the power of a country as great as America, can be in the hands of non elites.

What a coincidence, this chunk of viewer base, belongs again, to the Fox news and the talk radio. And who better to represent this viewer base, than Sarah Palin?

The most anti intellectual, the most dishonest and the most divisive figure in the history of American politics, who sells phony patriotism and phony worship of founding fathers, in her rallies. Needless to say, the most uninformed person on a national scene, to hold a public office.

John McCain probably did not know, how shallow and polarizing she was, when he picked her as a VP choice. He had spoken to her for only 15 minutes, before selecting her as a VP choice. And now, he is too much of a gentle man, to concede on the reality.

But as soon as she came into prominence, after the 2008 elections, Fox news hired her as a political analyst, and tried to make her the face of the main stream Republican Party. Portrayed her as a person, who was the victim of the mainstream and liberal media. A shining object that attracted more uninformed, ignorant, narcissist viewers, who are just looking for excuses, to be hateful towards the liberal America.

This gave rise to a new era of "anti intellectualism".

Sarah Palin, is just one example. There are Michele Bachmanns, Herman Cains, Donald Trumps and many more.

In this new era, it was OK not to believe in science, facts and academic success. To go a step beyond, it was ok to mock a Harvard Law Professor for being an elite. Everything he says, is called lecturing. On one hand, openly calling for worshipping the founding fathers of the country, completely ignoring the fact that the founding fathers were the liberal elites, and mostly the law professors.

Giving saint hood to Ronald Reagan and then criticizing Obama, for actually following the Reagan policies. And that too, for factually being on the further right of Reagan. For example, Sarah Palin criticized Obama for the policy, of reducing nuclear war heads down to 300. Not knowing that Reagan was for zero nuclear war heads, even in the height of the cold war. Accusing Obama for throwing Israel under the bus, when Reagan actually denounced Israel in the UN, for the air strikes on Iraq.

The next step in this era was to incite people, towards crossing the line, by using invidious terms like a "gangster government", "taking our country back", "needing a revolution". Suggesting it was OK to take guns to the Presidential rallies. Suggesting it was OK to put gun cross hair icons on the districts, you want defeated. Tragically, one of the districts included the district of Gabby Giffords, who actually ended up being shot.

And according to the Fox news and talk radio, Sarah Palin was the victim, for being criticized, for putting the cross hair signs, on the American map.

This anti intellectualism is a new feather in the cap for the GOP. Needless to say again, it is driving even the moderate Republicans away, let alone the independents. Such a party can never win a Presidential election.

Freedom of Speech is great, but there is not a single country in the world, where so much deliberation has gone into spreading, the misinformation, spreading anti intellectualism, and intentionally causing the division within the country and within the party.

Damage to the demographics:

As the 2012 elections were approaching, Obama was passing targeted legislations, one by one, to appeal to his individual constituencies, using compassionate language. Republican extremism and the conservative media world, was doing exactly the opposite, of driving them away, one by one, through incendiary language.

When the Presidential nominee of the party says, I would ask illegal immigrants to self deport, I will veto the dream act and I will not allow tuition fee waivers to the kids, who are in this country by no fault of their own, you know the party wants to drive away the Hispanics and the immigrants, purely based on just the tone, if not the policy.

Under President Obama, the highest number of illegal Mexicans are deported, and the least number of them, entered the United States. And yet, he has been able to grow his support among the Latinos, to the historic levels. The reason is, while strong action is being taken on the illegal immigrants, soft tone and sensible legislations, like 'The Dream Act' were implemented by Obama.

The goal here was to appeal to the Latino community, through the balanced and common sense approach. In two areas, key to this voter block. Firstly, projecting himself strongly, for the middle class and it's securities, where majority of the Hispanic voter base is. Secondly, showing sensitivity to the innocent younger generation of Hispanics, who are in the US by no fault of their own. 85% of the Americans, let alone Hispanics, agreed with 'The Dream Act'.

Republicans first, could project themselves strongly only for the "job creators", and then projected them selves as hostile opponents, of all illegal immigrants. Through their hysterical media and all throughout the GOP primaries.

To start with, some members of the Republican party and their mouth pieces in the media, have not separated all Hispanics from the illegal immigrants.

Embracing the Arizona immigration law 'Arizona SB 1070' so passionately, is a prime example. The law, that allows police to stop anyone, on the suspicion of being an illegal, and ask them for their documents. Clearly, this is color driven. Very little, this law will affect the illegal immigrants but will irate Hispanics, if they are questioned based on their looks. Because the majority of the Hispanics, are the first generation or the second generation citizens. And to vouch for this law, to be a national model, is nothing short of political suicide, with the Hispanic voters.

Some Republicans and media people are also projecting to their voter bases, that giving amnesty to illegal immigrants, is same as pampering to the Hispanic population. In short, suggesting that every Hispanic, has something to do with illegal immigration. This is offensive to Hispanics as well.

Granted, Hispanics will always sympathize with the illegal immigrants, but the main issue among Hispanics is the middle class struggle. GOP has not been effective in communicating their concern for the middle class. Tying Hispanics with illegal immigrants is the only message of cluelessness, comes across from the GOP.

And even if some in the GOP, tried to separate Hispanics from illegal immigrants, the rhetoric towards illegal immigrants, was so vitriolic in the primaries, that Hispanics, who will always feel some sympathy towards the illegal immigrants, are bound to feel hostility towards the entire party, if not some candidates.

Clearly, the rationalists in the Republican Party are not in the favor of this kind of rhetoric, given that the Hispanics are the single largest growing voter block. They are playing an increasingly important role in the states like Florida, Colorado and Nevada, which GOP has to win, to be able to have any legitimate shot at the Presidency.

In addition, if you analyze the other Asian voter blocks like Indians and Chinese; they are mostly a first or a second generation immigrants. They will always sympathize with the immigrants and understand their need to stay in this country, by all means.

After all, this is the country of immigrants and one can argue that the parents of some founding fathers by definition, were also the "illegal immigrants" in the land of native Americans.

Ronald Reagan was for Amnesty. George Bush and Karl Rove were very sensitive to Latinos, winning 44% of the vote in 2004. Jeb Bush also has openly conceded that the current GOP needs to change the attitude towards the Hispanics.

Fox news and talk radio know this very well, too.

This is exactly why Fox news strongly started defending the Arizona immigration law, which as mentioned above, is nothing short of racial discrimination and hostility towards the Hispanics.

This is exactly why we started seeing Arizona governor Jan Brewer, who is a big supporter of this law, time and again on Fox news. This is exactly why we saw, Arizona police officers appearing on the Fox news, defending this law. This is exactly why we saw, the Republican Party candidates being asked on Fox, if they supported the Arizona immigration law.

Intentions were clear. Defend Arizona immigration law, and drive away Hispanics.

Candidates also took pride in saying that English should be the official language of government in America.

As an outcome, in the Republican primaries, there was a race between the GOP candidates to outscore each other on how they are going to be tough on illegal immigrants. Rick Perry was booed for granting tuition fee waivers to Latino kids. Gingrich was slammed for suggesting that he will not deport grandma, by breaking a Latino family. Herman Cain got away with saying, I will put electric fence between the borders. This is exactly why Mitt Romney, the eventual nominee, had to take the positions he took in primaries. Not by his own choice.

Does Romney really believe, in whatever he had to say, in the primary debates? I don't think so. But he had to show, he was tough on illegal immigrants, to prove that he was severely conservative.

As a result, President Obama, despite doing nothing on the comprehensive immigration reform, despite deporting record number of Mexicans, led Mitt Romney by 50 points among Latinos. This was a record margin. Again, this was against Massachusetts moderate, Mitt Romney, whose father was born in Mexico.

Not once, Romney could relate his father's initial middle class struggle, including the arrival from Mexico and successfully pursuing American dream, to the largest growing voting block of Latinos. The voting block, that can so easily relate to Romney's father's back ground. Very unfortunate indeed for Romney.

Had Romney won the same amount of Latino vote that George Bush won in 2004, he would be the President.

Isn't this a serious retrogression and that too in such a short time, for the GOP?

Similarly, when Obama proposed that Catholic institutions should provide the contraception to the women, Fox news though their mouth pieces, waged this as a war on religion, with the extreme rhetoric. This gave Obama almost a 20 point advantage among women voters, against Romney, a loving family man who was married for 42 years.

Further, the younger generation believes in marriage equality for gays and women's right to choose. In short, people aligning themselves with religious beliefs, as well, are declining in numbers. And if you make the candidates like Rick Santorum, the symbols of conservatism, it is bound to expedite the isolation of GOP, from every voter group, other than white religious older men.

African Americas are driven away, primarily because of the fact that Obama is African American. But the invidious remarks, with racial hints like the food stamp President, questioning his faith and birth, have been on the rise, made Obama look like a victim. In addition, tactics like voter suppression have been implemented by the GOP, for the lower turn out among the African Americans. All these factors collectively, added fuel to the higher turn outs among African Americans. Higher turn outs than in 2008, when they had a historic, first black Presidential candidate. The reason is, this 2102 higher turnout was against the GOP, a lot more than for Obama.

In short, over the last few years, Fox news and talk radio together, with the extreme GOP candidates, have successfully driven away almost all voter groups, except white men and married white families. They have further locked the Republican Party, with the flawed and extreme candidates, who represented GOP, in the primaries.

If the white people were a growing voter block in America, this model would certainly have been beneficial. But in reality, quite the opposite it true. It is the minorities and the immigrants, who are growing in numbers. Precisely why, the future of the GOP is in jeopardy and that too for the long term.

Because of these polarizing GOP mouth pieces, women, blacks, Hispanics, immigrants, Jews, homosexuals and younger voters are now overwhelmingly voting, not only for the Democratic Party, but also with an additional impetus, of voting against the Republican Party.

To summarize, the GOP has been hurt in the three areas; values, intellect and demographics, antagonizing the moderate and independent America.

In reality, this neither represents the majority of the GOP politicians, nor the majority GOP voter base. However, Fox news, talk radio and the Tea Party bullies, have managed to give their vitriolic image to the entire party, making the establishment figures in the party, look anemic.

This always keeps a Democrat in the White House. This is good for the "class war fare", "wealth distribution" "bad government" and "socialism" rhetoric. And importantly, the top selling talking point; that unlike the biased, liberal lame stream media, we are the only fair and balanced network, that is being tough on the President.

Today, I don't think any GOP candidate has the courage to disagree with a Fox news analyst openly. Let alone denouncing. On the contrary, the candidates are probably scared to death, because of the possible bad mouthing that can come from Fox news, including from the side show clown pack, led by Donald Trump.

This is how the GOP has capitulated to Fox news and talk radio, causing severe decadence to their national appeal and strength. As a result, the Republican

Primaries were essentially, an unprecedentedly embarrassing reality show.

This has helped no one but Barack Obama enormously, and it played a big role in his 2012 reelection.

The most ingenious part about this damage is that, it is very intentional, well planned and extremely well executed, by Fox news and talk radio. And so is the division carried out, within the Republican Party. Hence the term, genius.

An evil genius of the cunning Fox.

6) How they brought down Romney

In 2012, the GOP could not have been more fortunate to have a candidate like Mitt Romney. A moderate Republican, which is a very dangerous combination for the Democrats. In a bad economy, with no other President ever winning with unemployment so high, GOP had a candidate who was one of the most successful and reputed businessmen, having turned around the failing Olympics, being a successful governor of a liberal state, where he worked with 87% of the opposition party members and passed the universal health care law. Not to mention, a great family man, who has donated millions to the charity, and has given two years of his life to the missionary cause. And most importantly a candidate, who could raise more money (including the super packs money), than Obama did.

This Massachusetts moderate Mitt Romney brought the following strengths, to the general election.

He was leading Obama among independents by double digits. In 2008, Obama lead McCain by 8 points. All the way till the election day, Romney led Obama on the most important question of the election, 'who was the better candidate for the economy'? These two reasons should have been enough for Romney to win. Add to which, the fact that enthusiasm among the Republican voters, was higher than the Democratic voters.

Further, Romney neither had the baggage of being a member of the Bush administration, nor being a member of the negatively viewed Republican congress. Additionally, he led Obama on the question, who can change the Washington. He was a much desired Washington outsider, a huge plus in these anti Washington sentiment times. And Romney was always going to ignite the passion in the conservative base, like never before, simply based on the fact that he was going to run against Barack Obama. A person, who the conservatives despised to the core. More than any previous Democratic candidate. And that too, in the middle of the anti incumbent trend, world wide.

Based on what he had to offer by himself, Romney should have won in a landslide. But quite the opposite happened. He lost by a landslide. Because, Mitt Romney had a baggage. The baggage of the Republican Party.

Mitt Romney's biggest enemy was not Barack Obama, not the class war fare, not the dislike among conservative voters, and not even the Mormonism. It was the hostility and the extremism in the Republican Party. The party that was taken over by Fox news, talk radio and the spiritual leaders of the Tea Party.

They systematically and step by step, destroyed Romney's every advantage and dragged him to the defeat, by loading him up with each and every of the Republican Party's disadvantages.

Starting with a direct verbal barrage, from some conservative figures, who were hell bent on labeling Romney a non-conservative. Irrespective of his record in Massachusetts. If they really wanted Romney to beat Obama, and if they thought he was not a conservative, they should have left the subject alone.

Why make it a big issue?

Following is what Ann Coulter said about Romney at the biggest conservative convention CPAC. "If Christie doesn't Run, Romney will be nominated and will lose". Following is what Rush Limbaugh has said, many times on his show, "Romney is not a conservative", "Moderates will lose in a land slide against Obama", knowing all along, that Romney was always going to be the nominee. Most importantly, knowing deep down very well, that only a moderate Republican can win a general election, by appealing to all communities, in such highly changed demographics.

These are the same talk show hosts and analysts, who gave saint hood to Ronald Reagan, who was a "Hollywood liberal", a California governor, who raised taxes a few times and added to the national deficit.

This is exactly why in the GOP primaries, Romney had to take the extreme and uncompromising positions, so that he can prove himself to be a "severely conservative" candidate, as he called himself at the CPAC speech. This kept on driving independents, moderates and minorities away.

Next, the conservative world, kept on pushing him hard for being a flip flopper, on the core and sensitive issues of abortion, gay marriage, guns and health care mandates, which also drove conservatives away, who did not like him in the first place.

Romney's primary opponents were Michele Bachmann, Rick Perry, Newt Gingrich, Rick Santorum, Herman Cain. The Tea Party favorites. Majority of the independents and moderate Republicans, called them clowns and deservedly so. A bunch of utterly incompetent, uninformed and polarizing figures, compared to Romney. No national appeal, and atrocious polling numbers against Obama.

Instead of discrediting these candidates, Fox news gave these candidates the credibility and the voices. This forced Romney to bear the brunt of attacks from these candidates. And the attacks from these candidates, were as negative as the ratings of these candidates. For example, Romney being called a vulture capitalist, a person who bankrupted companies, a hypocrite, a liar and so on. Even Obama's language in the general election, was nowhere close to this harsh.

Unfortunately, Romney had to step down to this bottom of the barrel, to defend him self. Also, had to pretend to look like one of them, and outpace them, with the positions, that could never be defended in the general election. For example, positions like veto the 'Dream Act', or sign the ban on 'Roe v Wade'. Anyone with common sense knows that these are not Romney's core beliefs. These positions drove Romney's negatives sky high, and gave a lot of material and red meat to Obama team.

If Fox news really cared for Romney's victory, they had the power to easily discredit the other primary candidates, who had no chance of winning the general election. Instead, what they did was put cynical and utterly divisive analysts like Sarah Palin, in charge of expressing opinions on Romney's credibility. His credibility as a true conservative.

Seriously, does Sarah Palin have a credibility to judge a self made, successful, brilliant person and a businessman like Romney?

I remember, in 2010, when Christine O'Donnell won the senate primary in Delaware, Karl Rove openly said that this is a nutty candidate and this will cost us the senate seat, that GOP should have won. Guess who backed Christine O'Donnell? The Fox news contributor Sarah Palin, against Karl Rove's opinion. As expected, Christine O'Donnell lost. GOP did not gain the control of the senate. Sarah Palin and Fox news had the capacity to stop Christine O'Donnell. But they did not.

Again, during the GOP primaries, Sarah Palin said, she voted for Newt Gingrich (over Mitt Romney), the most polarizing candidate, with the highest negative ratings ever. The reason she gave was, to keep the primaries going, so that the candidates can mature. This was the best thing that could have happened for Obama. Primaries kept on driving Romney's negatives up, as he was being burned by strong rhetoric of Gingrich. Deep down, Fox news and Sarah Palin both knew, not in the wildest of dreams, Newt Gingrich had a slightest of chance, of beating Obama.

Obama/ Hilary primaries as well, went deep and became personal. But they were the primaries, between the two intellectuals and two likable candidates. At the end of these primaries, approvals of Obama and Hilary had gone up. More people were excited about the candidates, than ever before in the history. Quite the opposite was true for the Republican primaries. Romney's negatives went sky high, and the primary turnout was historically down for him. In some cases, even lower than in his own turn out of 2008 primaries, when he lost to McCain. Romney had to outspend a candidate, as flawed as Rick Santorum, ten times to win his own home state of Michigan.

Why? Because Romney was a "Massachusetts Moderate"; like that was a bad thing. The Massachusetts literacy rate, the standard of schools, the percentage of uninsured, should make the red states (majority of them ranking among the poorest in America) envy of Massachusetts. Shouldn't Fox news and talk radio be praising Massachusetts, to be looked upon as a model for improvement, for the red states? The red states which get lot more of the federal money, than they contribute to?

And most importantly, has anyone at Fox, really analyzed Romney's record as a governor? He has been more conservative "by record" than Paul Ryan. Paul Ryan, who for no reason, gets a free label of being a true conservative, despite having an atrocious voting record on spending programs, without paying for them.

Next hurtful thing that Fox news has been doing is, to give an unlimited talk time to idiotic Donald Trump, the champion of the birther issue. How can anyone make, this self promoting, pompous and bombastic, entertainment in chief, credible? He is on Greta Van Sustern's show almost every week. Needless to say, Romney had to run around trying to get Donald Trump's endorsement. Or else, God knows what Donald and his giant ego, will say about Romney's credibility on Fox. How will this not drive the independents away? Making Donald Trump, an integral part of the Republican Party voices, has contributed a lot, to adding an image of the party, as a non-serious party. A "stupid" party, as being labeled by some of their own, after the election loss. And the image of the candidates, who were running for Trump's endorsement, came across as nothing but Pathetic.

But this was not enough. The most effective tactic was the targeted take down of Romney, by the Fox news anchors.

Guess who talked the most, about Romney's flip flopper label? And that too, in front of the national audience. Two of Fox's least partisan, moderate and the most credible anchors, Bret Baier and Chris Wallace.

Bret Baier, in the Conchita Food Ware House interview asked Romney, "Your critics charge that you make your decisions based on political expediency and not core conviction. You have been on both sides of some issues and there is video tape of you going back few years, speaking about different issues; climate change, abortion, immigration, gay rights. How can voters trust, what they hear from you today, is what you believe if you win the White House"?

What a remarkable question to a person, whom you want to be the next President.

After Romney's answer, he kept on pressing, "I am sure you have seen these ads using video tapes of you, in previous years speaking on various issues. And it seems like, it is in direct contrast to positions you take now". Romney tried to answer, by suggesting that it is Democratic attack, but Bret kept on pressing using names like John Huntsman. Then he pressed Romney hard on immigration, where Romney had taken an extreme position, as well. Further, he went after Romney for health care mandate, which everyone on this planet knows, that the conservatives immensely despise.

Finally, Romney had to call it an "unusual interview" in the middle of it. Romney did not call any other interview "unusual" on any other network. Later on, Bret Baier went on to the biggest Fox news daily show of Bill O'Reilly, and said publicly that "Romney was irritated by the interview and according to Romney, I (Bret) was overly aggressive. Then Romney came back from his holding room and said, he did not like the interview and it was uncalled for".

To be honest, firstly, it was shocking to see Romney attacked so decisively on Fox, and secondly, Bret Baier declaring the interview 'after math' publicly. One would imagine, Fox news would be the last one to do so. Real intentions were, to drive away the Fox news viewers from Romney at the polls.

In the Fox news GOP debate, the other level headed anchor, Chris Wallace went after Romney in the following words, "Some of your critics say that every one of these moves is for the political advantage. When you were running in MA you took liberal positions, when running for President, you are taking conservative positions. Is that Principle or is that just politics?"

Why such a strong language, that no other network used against Romney?

Then he kept on pressing Romney, on gun rights and gay marriage, the issues which are very sensitive to the conservative audience. The audience that does not trust Romney anyways.

Later again, it was in the FOX news GOP debate, Bret Baier asked the candidates to raise their hands for

$10 in spending cuts to $1 in tax increase. Isn't this an independent voter killer? There was no way a GOP candidate would have raised hand for the tax increase, in the GOP primaries. Fox news knows this. But the goal was to trap them on a video tape, in front of national audience, as uncompromising candidates, even for a $10 of spending cut. This is why Fox did not choose a smaller, but more realistic figure like $5, for spending cut. In reality, there was never going to be a proposal, by any Democrat for a $10 in spending cuts to $1 in tax increase.

This stance was used time and again against Romney, in his talking points by Obama, in the general election. This was purely a trap set for Romney, to make him look, a non compromising, right wing extremist. Again by no other network, but Fox news.

This is called throwing the Presidential candidate under the bus.

Collectively, all factors considered, no other network was so harsh and damaging to Romney. Not even the lame stream media. Can you imagine anyone at MSNBC, being so harsh to their candidate, President Obama?

Can you imagine, what kind of 30 second ad material, these kind of interviews, from Fox would give to Obama for the general election? Romney's image as a bad corporate raider, a flip flopper and a non compromising right wing extremists, was readily made by the GOP primary contenders, with the help of Fox news and talk radio. This was a gift that was handed over on a silver platter, to the class war fare lion's den, of Obama's billion dollar general election campaign, that was parked in the battle ground states for the 4 years.

When Sandra Fluke took a center stage, during the women's contraception issue, all Romney and the centrist Republicans had to do, was not talk about this issue. And quite smartly, they did not. But then, Rush Limbaugh called Sandra Fluke a slut.

Obama quickly jumped in to console Sandra Fluke and Romney was thrown into the fire, to separate himself from Rush Limbaugh. Romney, who already has an issue, of being labeled as a moderate, by the conservative media, obviously could not denounce Rush Limbaugh, a more trusted figure in the conservative world. Clearly, a losing proposition for Romney either way, for no fault of his own.

Does any level headed person really believe that Romney, who has been married to his high school sweet heart for 40+ years, and has raised a great family, is against women's rights? But again, it is Rush Limbaugh's party that had put him at a disadvantage, among the biggest voter block women, and that too by an irreparable margin.

With all these interviews and events, anyone who believes that Fox news and talk radio, really had any interest in Romney Presidency, is sleeping. Last 4 years of high viewership, high ratings and millions of dollars in revenues, are too much of a charity, to give away, for the next 8 years of Romney Presidency.

Romney had lost the Presidential election, even before the general election campaign began.

Now that finger pointing and soul searching has begun, for the Republican Party, they need to start pointing fingers at the real culprits, who have given them this division and the extreme image. And the real soul searching would be to gather the courage, to stand up to the extremism, cynicism and the anti intellectualism, propagated by the Fox news, talk radio and company.

7) Definition of a bad politician

If one starts analyzing and dissecting Paul Ryan's Republican National Convention speech, perhaps that person will have to write a separate book, just to cover all the distortions and lies from that speech.

For the first time, in this book I will be using strong language against someone, because there is no other way to describe Paul Ryan.

Cynicism, obviously exists on both sides of the isle but some politicians, just exceed all limits of it. They have no morals, no convictions. Sometimes, I wonder if they ever feel guilty, at least in their own eyes, about their own character! Or they lack even that much basic moral clarity! In this category of politicians, Paul Ryan stands head and shoulders above anyone.

George Bush and Dick Cheney have taken a lot of criticism, for their policies and mistakes. But one creditable thing about Bush/Cheney is that they had convictions, and stood by their voting records, no matter what. More importantly, unlike Paul Ryan, they never blamed opposition party for their own faults.

Consider an example of a goon, who stabs someone and causes that person to bleed. Then blames the doctor, for not stopping the bleeding enough. Next, asks for being put in charge of the patient, for stopping the remaining recovery of the patient. Paul Ryan is like this goon. In reality, I think even these goons have higher morals than Paul Ryan. They would probably just stab the patient, and walk away.

Between years 2000-2008, Paul Ryan voted for both the wars. Did not bother to pay for them. Voted for Bush tax cuts and did not worry, if they were deficit neutral, no matter what CBO said. Voted for

Medicare prescription drug program, that produced the largest overhaul of Medicare, in the public health program's 38-year history. Did not worry about paying for it. Voted for the first $700 billion plus, TARP/ bank bailout under Bush, without paying for it. And then, he was one of the very few Republicans, who also voted for the first auto bailout under Bush. This accounts for approximately 5 trillion dollars of new spending programs.

However, as soon as Obama was sworn in, Paul Ryan became "fiscally conservative".

Felt that he had the moral obligation, to criticize Obama for the national debt, to which he himself had a lot bigger contribution, than Obama did.

All of a sudden, he started worrying about the government spending, government interference, wastage of tax payer dollars, out of hand entitlement spending and so on and so on.

After voting for the patriot act, he now started talking about the individual liberty.

In short, after being an integral part of a bad 2000-2008 government, in 2009, he started saying government is bad.

For some reason, Paul Ryan is a true conservative and a favorite of Fox news, talk radio and the Tea Party. In short, the people who stand for less government, people who hate the government spending, borrowing money and national debt. Again, goes down to the ignorance, partisanship and the dislike of the President of the opposition party.

Forget Obama, Paul Ryan gets to be more conservative than even Mitt Romney, who actually balanced the budget in Massachusetts!

The epitome of hypocrisy came in Ryan's acceptance speech, at the Republican Convention Speech, when he talked about a GM plant being closed. He said that candidate Obama, promised that this plant will not close, if the Govt is there to help. But the plant got closed. What he did not say, is that the plant closed before Obama took office and Paul Ryan was a part of that government, under whom the GM plant actually closed.

How can tea party, which claims to be all about the American values, possibly like this immoral person?

Next came, one of the biggest hypocritical pandering of the American people. Ryan said in that speech, if you created a business, "you built that" (an Obama gaffe) but then said, "If you are feeling left out or passed by, you have not failed, your leaders have failed you".

This is nothing but deliberately keeping people in ignorance, and deliberately misleading them. Deliberately passing the blame, on to someone else that does not deserve it. In short, feeding poison against the government.

If you succeed, you get the credit but if you fail, government gets the blame. Needless to say, this blame was applicable only to the Obama government that took office in January 2009. Not the Ryan/ Bush government that was spending tax payer money, way more than Obama government did, and was forcing phony wars on the country, that killed our 3500 troops.

Paul Ryan's office sent 4 letters to President Obama's energy secretary, asking for the stimulus money. Letters stating, that he was pleased that the project would stimulate the economy, for his district. Admitting that one project, would create approximately 7600 jobs. In 2012 campaign, when this issue was brought out, Ryan said that he did not recall the letters. Even if they were signed by him (personally or rubber stamped by his office). But later, confessed that he takes personal responsibility for them, even if he would never ask for the stimulus money. How convenient?

Same Paul Ryan, was the most out spoken critic of the Obama stimulus of 2009. But deep down, he knew that the stimulus money works. As projected even by the non partisan Congressional Budget Office, no matter what the GOP, or the Fox news talking points say, about the stimulus.

Can there be a bigger hypocrite than Paul Ryan? How can tea party possibly like this coreless person? But the Tea Party, through their ignorance and hatred for the other side, has now learned to digest lies, as far as the liars, are running against Obama. You can be made to believe in anything, and you can be made to believe, out of anything.

Is this going to be the future of GOP?

Till we have partisan politicians like Paul Ryan, who want to rise in the party ranks, there will never be meaningful bipartisan achievements in the Washington.

This is where the second term of Obama comes into the picture. Actually, just a second term of any President is what Washington badly needed, in such a partisan atmosphere. Thankfully, America has got the second Presidential term. Perhaps, the Paul Ryans will start thinking about the betterment of the country.

Obviously, not for their dedication to the country, but at least for the future of their party. At least, for winning the future Presidential elections.

8) Stand up GOP

81% people polled outside the US, wanted Obama to win the 2012 elections. Just 19% wanted Romney, a charitable and loving family man. Now, this may have a lot to do with Obama's rock star popularity, but to believe that as a sole reason, for the world's choice, is a howler.

Why did Republican Party lose two straight land slide Presidential elections, with Obama getting more than 330 electoral votes? Why did they lose, the American popular vote, in the last 5 out of 6 Presidential elections? Answer is simple. They are not popular among the majority. Not in the US and not in the world. How did Ronald Reagan's party, that still talks about Reagan, as if he is their previous President, is winning the unpopularity contest, so convincingly?

Over 60% of people in America believe that top 1% should pay more taxes. Over 70% of the people believe that America should not be in wars. Over 60% of the people believe that abortion should be a personal choice. And over 60% of the people believe in some kind of legal path forward, to the illegal immigrants.

The stubborn policy stances taken by, or made to be taken by the GOP candidates, on these issues, are not resonating with the majority of the American people.

This is exactly why, so many times, people saw Mitt Romney flip flopping, on so many of the issues. Not Romney's fault.

No President had ever won the reelection since FDR, with unemployment above 7 %. Guess what, Obama just did and that too with a land slide.

In 2008, America saw an unprecedented Obama coalition of young voters, Hispanics, women, Asians and blacks. Everyone called it, a first time charm. To everyone's surprise, this coalition just got lot stronger in 2012, to the dismay of GOP.

Over the next 4 years, Obama is going to make this coalition even stronger. For his party and for this successor. Either Biden or Hilary, to both of whom he is enormously indebted to. Both of them already have a much broader national appeal than any GOP candidate on the horizon, may be with an exception of Jeb Bush.

For the first time, in a long time, Obama's Democrats have a huge advantage over the Republicans, even on the issue of foreign policy. Specially, Hilary Clinton.

Once reliable, big Republican States like Florida, Virginia, Colorado, Nevada and Ohio, have now become toss ups. Bush won them all in 2004. But GOP could not win a single one of them, in 2008 as well as 2012, against the Obama demographics. With increase in Latino and immigrant population, by 2020, they will become safely Democratic states. And no matter how weak, the Democratic candidate is, GOP will have no hopes of winning Presidency ever.

This is very bad for the country. Not just for the GOP.

If the invincibility is granted to any one party (The Democratic Party in this case), for the Presidency, that party starts serving it's own interest, instead of the common good. They keep people addicted to entitlements, and pamper them to keep the voter base locked. This is the reason, why America needs GOP to be a powerful party. A party which has the capacity to win the Presidential elections. A party that can appeal to majority of Americans, which obviously includes, appealing to minorities, moderates and independents.

Bottom line, the GOP has a mountain to climb and there are no easy fixes or the workarounds. Real and long term solution is needed. A positive solution.

Laura Ingraham, a conservative talk radio show host, said the following just before the 2012 elections, about the GOP "If you can not beat Barack Obama with this record, then shut down the party. Shut it down. Start new, with new people".

New People? On the same path? Dead wrong.

What GOP needs is a new path, a new set of inclusive policies, moderation and more importantly the likability.

In short, a turnaround of 180 degrees, that starts with discrediting Laura Ingraham.

Align the party with what the majority of the nation wants. Bring awareness into the voter base about the changing country, and the need for the change. Also, talk about the consequences of not changing, even if you don't like this change. Reality is a bitter pill to swallow, but swallowing the pill, would be better than seeing a life time of Democrat, in the White House.

Most importantly, the voters need to be told that they don't have to compromise on their principles in the personal life. But they will have to let their party compromise, on the principles and stances that their party takes. The reason is, the principles and stances of the majority of America, have changed.

What GOP needs is few national party spokes people and leaders, who are genuinely moderate, likable and who can stand up to all the bullies, of anti intellectualism, division and cynicism.

They don't really need to go beyond their party for this. For example, just study John Huntsman. A moderate, a progressive and yet a candidate having a very conservative track record. More importantly, a person who appears and sounds believable, while being a moderate, a progressive and a conservative. Naturally, a very likable candidate, even when you don't agree with him.

The only candidate who told Mitt Romney, that it is my duty to answer the President's call to serve his cabinet, even if he is the Democratic President. Person, who criticized Mitt Romney, for being against the bi partisanship.

But in the primaries, he was the second one to drop out; way before the majority of the clown pack. This speaks to the immaturity of the misinformation filled, voter base. The voter base, which did not see his record, a truly conservative record. Perhaps, one can say that the voter base was never told about this record.

This voter base needs to be educated. Instead, Laura Ingraham, Fox news and talk radio are doing exactly the opposite. Keeping the voter base in dark and deception.

Tea Party was formed after Obama took office. Naturally they did not like him from the get go, without much logic. Even if the Tea Party led the GOP landslide of 2010, in the 2012 Presidential elections, the GOP Presidential candidate was severely damaged, because of the Tea Party backed primary opponents.

Thanks to the 2010 Tea Party darlings, Sharron Angle and Christine O'Donnell, Harry Reid is still not only in the Senate, but is also a Senate Majority leader. In 2012, he is the Senate Majority leader by a wider margin, again thanks to Tea Party backed Todd Akin and company.

About time, someone in the GOP brings the Tea Party to real senses and tells them the reality. If not for the betterment of the country, at least for the better future of the Republican Party.

That does not mean, GOP should denounce the Tea Party. They just need to educate them. GOP needs the Tea Party. The Tea Party that is sensible and cooperative. Not the current version, of the hostage taking uncompromising Tea Party.

I am sure that Fox news, talk radio and some selfish Tea Party leaders will stand in the way. Because this moderation and education of the voters, hurts their cynical interests, strategies and eventually revenues.

Hence the GOP has no other option but to stand up to them. The reason is, now it has come down to the life and death scenario for the party. If they can not stand up to the Fox news, talk radio and the extremists in the Tea party, not in the wildest of dreams, they can stand up to Barack Obama's Democratic party and it's super coalition, as they saw in 2012.

I am optimistic that GOP will start fighting this extremism. This fight may last for the first year or so, but will help the GOP long term. Extremists will tone down. The extremists have nowhere else to go, but the GOP. In the end, they will have to come along. But if the GOP does not fight this extremism, they will look weak and flip floppers like Romney did. And they will never win the national popularity, in this changed nation.

On the contrary, if they really stand up to these extremist forces and take them on, like what Chris Christy does, these extremists will squeal like pigs. And in fact independents, and even some moderate Democrats, will find it appealing, for them to consider the GOP candidates. Again, like they are attracted by Chris Christy.

My personal feeling is that, had Mitt Romney stood up to Rush Limbaugh and denounced him on the Sandra Fluke slut comment, lot more women and Independent voters, would have found Romney appealing, strong and likable.

Republicans may not like Mitt Romneys, but they are the only ones who can win the general election. The reason is, they can attract the independents, and don't drive away the moderates. Sarah Palin, Michele Bachmann and Rick Santorum can not. The reason is that entire America does not hate Barack Obama, or the liberal America, like the Fox news, talk radio and the Tea party audience does.

Making Barack Obama, a one term President, was GOP's wish, and there was nothing wrong with that wish. But to make him a one term President was the choice of the entire nation. Not just the GOP voters. GOP certainly has the capability to appeal to the entire nation. The ball needs to start rolling fast.

Republican Party has a lot of positives, which attract independent and moderates. For example being against the entitlement society, being for less government spending, being for balancing budget, being for pro business, entitlement reforms, being for more power to the states, etc. What GOP has to articulate is, how all of these principles, the conservative principles, are in favor of the common man, instead of just the rich people. Something that Ronald Reagan could do.

Show that appealing to minorities like Hispanics, is not all about immigration but it is about being for middle class securities, like the health care coverage and education.

Concentrate on only one message. How, your conservative policies are going to be better, than the Democratic policies, for the economic interests of the middle class. For the protection of their basic necessities like health care, education, over the long term. Talk about investing in infrastructure more, than investing $2 billion more in defense spending, because not even a level headed child, in the "mainstream" America believes, that American military will be weak, as a result of cutting it by less than 5%.

The era of no tax increases for the rich, while cutting planned parenthood, teachers and firefighters is also gone. Because the Republicans just saw that the rich alone, can't win them elections. The common man does. The common man, who saw the need for the emergency workers and the government, in hurricane Sandy, just a week before the election.

Instead of talking about the bad government or no government, start talking about the efficient government.

Talk more about what you will do to cover the uninsured, than just talking about repealing

Obamacare. Because, the loss of health insurance is what a Hispanic and a middle class voter, worries about the most.

In short, the Republican Party needs to show that being a conservative party, and being an inclusive party are not mutually exclusive, unlike the party's current image. Communicate the message of growth and prosperity through openness and embracement, instead of austerity and heartlessness.

If the GOP can protect the interests of 'job creators', the phoniest term invented by a man kind, they can protect the interests, of a laid off worker. Or, at least talk about it.

GOP can simply find the answers to this dilemma in Ronald Reagan and George H W Bush. Both had the national appeal, because they were inclusive, progressive and moderate conservatives. And more importantly were "believably likable" to the entire nation.

George H W Bush, despite being a Texan, won states as liberal as California. And no matter how, the G W Bush Presidency is judged, even W did not appear to be a person, who was hostile to any community, unlike the current era of active conservatives.

Jeb Bush, for all we know, may be the person who can lead this much needed inclusive and moderate GOP recovery. His main task is to successfully fight the drag from the GW Bush Presidency, and change the image of the damaged party at the same time. Not an easy task, but four years is a long enough time to do so.

This task needs an urgent start.

Days of no compromise and strong language are over. For these next 4 years, what GOP needs is Obama's campaign slogan, 'Hope and Change'.

9) Political optimism

2012 Presidential election was going to be a turn out election. Americans knew the record of the two parties in the last two years. Democrats, as soon as they got into the power, knew that they are not going to get any bipartisan support from the other side. The other side knew that, if they give bipartisan support to Obama, for the economic recovery, and for solving the real issues facing the nation, he will be reelected. Hence both parties did what they had to do. Obama's accomplishments targeted his own base, and Republicans had no accomplishments, other than earning a reputation of 'party of no'. That means, playing the role of obstructionist, to the economic recovery, under the false pretence, of stopping the government spending. And then blame the lack of recovery on Obama. They counted on economy to get worse, and hoped that people will turn out against Obama, to vote for their candidate.

But their gamble did not work. Obama got reelected. In addition, the reputation of GOP has been tarnished significantly. One for being a non compromising, extremist party and two for being hostile to minorities. The reputation they earned though the primaries. In addition, there will be internal finger pointing and blame games, inside the GOP.

GOP will address all these issues going forward, by being positive. Also, now that Obama is reelected, they do not have to worry about making him a one term President either.

Obama as well, will not be worrying about only his reelection, like he did in the first term. He will be working towards solidifying his party image, as a party that has taken tough and bold decisions. For this purpose, he may have to take the short term blame, from his liberal base. But he won't mind, if it is going to benefit his successors, long term in 2016. And more importantly, if it is going to elevate his legacy. After all, he is the progressive President who is moving America forward, and wants to solve the big challenges facing the nation.

Considering 2016 elections, will not have an incumbent to run against, both parties have to earn the credibility and the goodwill for 2016. Both parties have to show the positive contribution to the economy. Specially, the Republicans who will have to do a lot better than just 6 years of obstructionism. Not waste time on futile symbolic idiocies, like repealing Obama care, Dream Act, Don't Ask Don't Tell and Dodd Frank.

Thankfully, under Obama, America has learned to fight the wars efficiently, without putting troops on the ground. Americans have also learned the hard price of fighting wars, to start with. Hence, in the future, there will not be any new wars waged, to show the opposition party, how strong the President is. There will not be new a boogeyman, created out of countries like Iran, to show the voters, how America stands behind Israel.

America's biggest problem is debt and spending and there is no substitute to reducing both. More importantly, there is no substitute to doing so, in a balanced and in a bipartisan way. The biggest spending programs and debt drivers are the Social Security, Medicare and the defense spending. Cutting these programs is like cutting a holy cow, for both the parties. Fortunately, they can blame it on the bipartisan commission of Simpson Bowles. Republican senators like Lindsey Graham, have already suggested adopting Simpson Bowles. And Obama as well, would like to take credit for creating this bi partisan commission, and adopting it to add to his legacy.

This will help the 2016 candidates of both the parties without the candidate, himself killing the holy cow.

What hurricane Sandy has taught us is that the global warming is real and we need better infrastructure. Embarrassingly enough, America currently ranks 22nd in the world in infrastructure. I really hope that America invests more in infrastructure, because it is just inconceivable, that a third world country like China has high speed rails and better highways, which America does not have. It is in the interest of both the parties to come up with these proposals, as infrastructure creates jobs as well.

This is why the second term of any President, not just Obama's, will be good for the bipartisanship and serious problem solving. Does not matter, even if it is for the selfish reasons of both the parties.

This is why the Democracy is so great. Political parties can be kicked out, for not performing.

10) American Supremacy

In his inaugural speech John F. Kennedy said the following famous line "My fellow Americans: ask not what your country can do for you--ask what you can do for your country"

America is not asking Americans to do anything for the country. All that Americans have to do is, ask themselves, what they can do for themselves. If Americans are willing to ask themselves such a simple question, then they have lot more to gain than anyone else in the world, because their country

America, still has lot more to offer than any other country in the world.

Again, by no means, I am suggesting that majority of Americans are not asking the question, "What they can do for themselves", and are not taking the individual responsibility. Of course they are. After all, they are the ones who built this great nation.

One of the pillars of American strength is the quality of education that is available to the people. It is available even in the low cost institutions, like community colleges, state universities, etc. It is one of the misconceptions in the western world, that the quality of education is extremely great in India and China. Specially in Math and Science, because of which, Indians and Chinese come to the US, and take American jobs.

In fact, the quality of education in premium Indian institutions is much worse, than what is available even in the ordinary universities in the US. For example, Bombay University, which I attended, is one of the premier universities in India. And when I came to California State University, Fresno, which can be considered an average school in the US, offered a drastically better standard of education, in all the subjects.

A person graduating from a university like California State University Fresno, will have a much better and in depth knowledge of the subject, compared to a person, coming from Bombay University. He will be in a much better position, to do an industry job or acquire higher education, in the same field.

Same goes for the professional industry. Besides the superior technology in the industry, there is just no comparison between the professionalism and the dedication with which, American workers perform their jobs, compared to the workers in countries like India, China. People in my country of birth, may criticize me for this statement, but that is just the reality.

Even the innovation aspect of the country, which can be attributed to the 'problem creation and problem solving' education culture of America, is far superior to countries like India and China. In fact, that part of the world has almost produced no major innovation, in the last couple of centuries.

The difference is, focus of the students. The top 5% of Indians and Chinese, which is a very large number, have actually realized what the American dream is. Despite going through the ordinary education system in their home countries, they select the career majors, which get them jobs in the west.

Obama is the only politician, who actually told the partial reality to a common person in the debate. And that too, perhaps because he was getting blamed for certain jobs, not being created in America. He said, "Some jobs are not just coming back". True. These are the jobs, which can be done anywhere in the world. Hence, they will be done in the places, where the cost is the cheapest possible. This is common sense and perfectly justifiable.

This new reality is now sinking in. Many Americans have already realized what the problem is. And they are on track to fix it. As I said earlier, they are the ones, who have built this great nation. I personally have a strong feeling that the next generation Americans, are going to focus a lot more on "job oriented" education, than focusing on selecting a major they like.

This is why, given America's strength in education system, innovation leadership and the best in class industry, America is well poised to be on track, for a very strong rebound. It will maintain it's clear superiority in the world, over the rest, and that too, for a long time.

It is just that this biased, hurtful media, and some of these opportunist politicians, that are causing this division and hindrance, have to get out of the way.

So that this great nation, as one people, can make full use of it's own potential.

The end

Influences

Joe Scarborough

'Morning Joe' is an extremely informative program that I watch religiously. Although, Joe Scarborough openly calls himself a conservative and a Republican, he never hesitates to criticize his own party and the candidates for their mistakes and record. Never fails to praise the Democrats and the Obama administration, when deserved. On the program, you get a fair analysis the daily happenings, where both parties stand, what problems our country is facing, and which way should be the road forward. Along with the co host, Mika Brzezinski and the daily panel contributors, 'Morning Joe' clearly is the best political program, on all the networks combined.

Fareed Zakaria

Fareed provides an in depth knowledge of the global affairs, America's interaction with the outside world and how America is positioned in the world, short term as well as long term. This information is very essential to the American common man. Additionally, his understanding of the Islamic world and America's complex relationship with the Middle East, makes him one of the most valuable media resources in the US. He was born in my home town of Mumbai India, which also has a big Muslim population. Countries like America, India and the ones in the Middle East, need more progressive Muslims like Fareed. His show, 'Fareed Zakaria GPS' and his book 'The Post American World' are a great source of knowledge.

John Huntsman

A Republican who said, America does not torture, America has made mistakes in the past, and working in the Obama administration was my duty to serve the nation. Clearly, his party was not ready for him. But they will be in 2016, given the shellacking they received, for abolishing all these common sense ideas, which Huntsman talked about. There was a reason, why some Obama administration insiders had suggested, that John Huntsman is a candidate who they feared the most. The reason is, he has a proven conservative record and yet he is a progressive, moderate Republican. He will appeal to the independents and the minorities. Him and Jeb Bush, are the only two people, who can probably lead the Republican come back.

Bill Maher

Considering he is a comedian, who hates the Republicans, mocks religion and calls America a dumb country, I should not be writing Bill Maher's name, in the list of influences. However, also considering the fact, that we are in the 21st century, and America is the most advanced nation in the world, there is enough ignorance in the certain segments of a common man, which needs to be highlighted and mocked. You may not agree with his style, but Bill Maher comes across as a person, who would not put partisanship ahead of the country, no matter how much he hates and mocks the other side. He treats Republicans respectfully on his show and engages with them, on a common sense level, than a partisan level. Importantly for me, he is a big supporter of environmental protection, and supporter of quality food and health standards, both extremely critical to the entire world, especially America.

Ron Paul

Even if Ron Paul's image comes across as an anti government extremists, he probably would have been the least damaging, as a President, for America. America's entire wealth and potential would have been concentrated on building America, and not the outside world, or the corporate interests. For sure, America would not be in the debt, had Ron Paul's principles would have been followed, going back to the dates, when America's entitlement programs started. His truthfulness and courage are both admirable. Even when the GOP primary contestants were cynically mocking him, at times when the crowd was booing him, he never wavered from his positions. Really admirable!

*M*y first day in the dream world

"1996 Olympics will be held in the city of Atlanta" I was 15 years old, when I heard this announcement on TV. I told my mom, how lucky my cousin sister is, who had just moved to Atlanta from New York.

Very little I knew, what lied ahead.

1:20 am Indian Standard Time, Aug 03, 1996. Six years later, Delta airlines saw the Mumbai, India coast off. I was leaving my home town for the land of opportunities, for the very first time, on student visa.

My cousin, whom I thought was lucky, made me feel lot more lucky when she told me, she had booked my tickets for the Olympics. My port of entry in the US was going to be the city of Olympics. My first day in US, was going to be the last day of Olympics. The last session of Olympics was going to start just two hours after my flight was supposed to land into the airport, an hour's train ride from the stadium. And being the final Olympics session, it was also going to be the grand finale session, which included the track finals, where US was one of the major contenders. It could not have been more theatrical for me.

And so began my journey, with a lot of excitement.

Even if I had planned, I did not get a chance to revise my broken German, which I dearly wanted to speak in my halt in Germany.

After a tiring Aug 02, my nap ended when my flight was above the enchanting Bavarian Alpine villages. Breathtaking small houses, curvy meticulous roads and crystal blue water lakes made me think, "I probably should have applied to schools in Germany and not the US". This was my first bird's eye view, of one of the world's greatest landscapes.

Had forgotten all about refreshing German and before I knew my flight landed into Frankfurt.

"Guten Tag, Ich Moechte nach Atlanta gehen" (Good morning, I would like to go to Atlanta), I bravely told the German Delta Airline officer in the transit area. He felt pity for my German and responded in English, "right this way". I thought he was not German. But he spoke fine German, with the person who followed me out.

Same was the story with an attendant in the book store. I quickly gave up on speaking in German.

After walking a few steps, I ran into an American, who looked very familiar. But I had never known an American before. Then I realized that he was the officer in American Consulate, who actually issued my Visa. Obviously I went to him and said hi.

He was surprised and said "quite a coincidence huh?" I said "Hell yeah". He further asked me, "Are you going to the games?" I replied "Yes. How about you"? He said "Unfortunately not". I joked, "You know, you could have stopped me from going". We both had a nice laugh and he said "have fun".

And then, the only thing that occupied my mind was the thought, of landing into the greatest country in the world, for the first time in my life. No immigrant can ever forget that feeling.

What would be more fun? Seeing America for the first time, or seeing the Olympics?

I had forgotten all about Germany on the Frankfurt airport itself.

Our flight took off for the land of "burger, fries and coke". With so much excitement in my mind, naturally it became a very long flight. Every minute felt like an hour. I don't think I have seen my watch so many times again in my life, ever. Luckily they showed a good Tom Hanks movie, BIG.

Movie killed important two hours. But that's it. No more breaks, just the long waiting game.

It felt like a year, before the flight finally landed into Atlanta. Because of the Olympics, the whole Airport was beautifully decorated. It looked like Buckingham palace. Security was also very tight (especially after a bomb blast, just two weeks back in Atlanta).

As I picked up my bags, a Police officer came to me with a small dog, perhaps a small pit bull. The dog looked adorable (like the dog in Men in Black II). He jumped on my bags, sniffed bags quickly and got down. "Good boy" said the officer and gave him a biscuit. Charming!!!

I was wondering, how we were going to drop all the bags home and then reach stadium in time. But my brother in law resolved that issue. He carried my bags home in his car, and me and my cousin sister, left for the Olympics.

Since it was going to be a long night, we decided to eat on the airport. "I need to buy something spicy for you" said my cousin and we bought Wendy's Spicy Chicken Sandwich. After eating it, we both laughed about how this sandwich is the spiciest in the US. "Better get used to it!!" said my cousin. Till date, this remains my most favorite burger in the US.

We took Atlanta's "Marta" to reach the stadium. I wanted to buy a coke. Put dollar in the wending machine, which was broken. Did not give me the coke and ate my dollar. This is how I spent my first dollar in the US. I bought coke from a small boy, who was selling the bottles from his backpack.

Once we entered the colossal stadium, the stage was set for track finals, javelin throw and women's high jump finals. US national team was one of the major contenders for the track finals. Once the races started, sixty thousand people got behind the team screaming "USA, USA, USA..............."

The atmosphere became even more electric, once the darkness took over.

Javelin throw competition was the pick of the events. We were quite fortunate, to be located at the receiving end of the throw. Once the colored Javelin was thrown up in the air in the dark, a powerful floodlight would follow it's trajectory, across the stadium and would land right below us.

I asked my cousin, "Can you please pinch me? I really don't know if this is a dream or not". Attending Asiad games in Delhi, looked like an improbable thing, when we were young. So, attending not only Olympics, but that too the track finals on the last day, in the country that was 10000 miles away, was certainly light years away, when I first heard about the Atlanta Olympics.

While coming back home, we got down from the train. My cousin told me, "will eat Varan bhat at home tonight (in my local language Marathi, lets eat curry and rice)". On the relatively empty station, we were quite loud. And one Indian fellow, from the distance screamed, "me pan yeu ka? (can I join too)" in Marathi, my local language.

I told my cousin, you know this day, already has been so dramatic, I am not surprised this person asked us this question in Marathi. We both had a laugh.

Finally we came to my cousin's newly decorated huge

American home. Cleaned up myself and got under the think comforter, in the cold Atlanta weather.

32 hours, after I said goodbye to my homeland, it was still August 03, the day that changed my residence and life for the next 15 years. I was finally in the land of the free and the home of the brave. The feeling was sinking in.

Lying on the bed, I thought, lets try to remember each and every experience I had today, starting from saying goodbye to folks 10000 miles away, to running into the Visa officer in Germany, to the bag sniffing dog, to Spicy chicken in Wendy's, to Marta and the Olympics.

But just could not do so. It was too overwhelming to remember. Was tired and slowly fell asleep, with the sound of 60000 people, still echoing in my ears.

My very first day in America, was a dream come true. This perhaps explains, why people in America say, "God bless America"!

Thank you for reading.

Shantanu Kamat